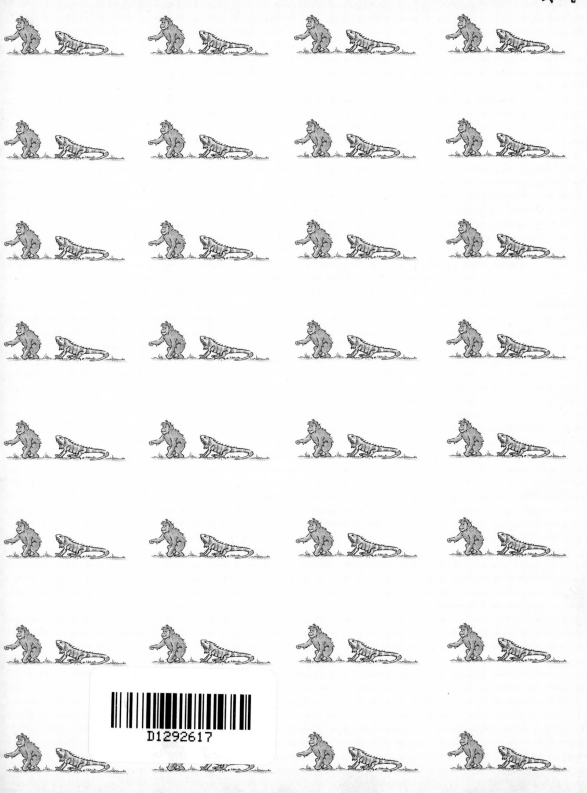

A DORLING KINDERSLEY BOOK

Written by Angela Royston
Photography by Philip Dowell
Additional Photography (pages 14-15 and 18-19) by Dave King
and (pages 12-13 and 20-21) by Jerry Young
Illustrations by Martine Blaney and Dave Hopkins
Animals supplied by Trevor Smith's Animal World

Eye Openers ™
First published in Great Britain in 1991
by Dorling Kindersley Limited,
9 Henrietta Street, London WC2E 8PS

Douglas & McIntyre Limited
585 Bloor Street West
Toronto, Ontario M6G 1K5

Canadian Cataloguing in Publication Data

Royston, Angela
Jungle animals

(Eyeopeners ; 7)
ISBN 0-88894-842-5

1. Jungle fauna - Juvenile literature. I. Title.
II. Series.

QL112. R68 1991   j591   C90-095652-6

Reproduced by Colourscan, Singapore
Printed and bound in Italy by L.E.G.O., Vicenza

·EYE·OPENERS·
Jungle
Animals

DOUGLAS & MCINTYRE

Monkey

This monkey lives in the jungle treetops. It uses its hands, feet, and tail to climb from branch to branch. Baby monkeys ride on their mothers' backs. Monkeys eat fruit, insects, and plants.

hand

face

tail

7

Jaguar

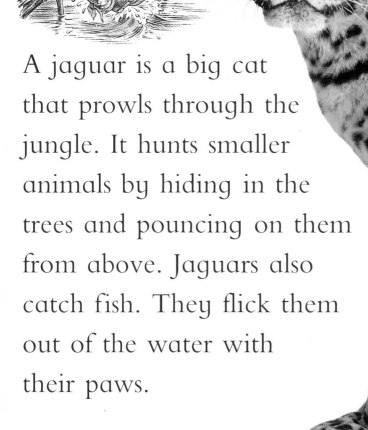

ear

A jaguar is a big cat
that prowls through the
jungle. It hunts smaller
animals by hiding in the
trees and pouncing on them
from above. Jaguars also
catch fish. They flick them
out of the water with
their paws.

fangs

tail

paw

9

Tree frog

leg

This tiny green tree frog is so small that it could sit on your thumb. It hides from its enemies among the green leaves. Tree frogs have sticky fingers and toes. They cling to leaves and twigs, looking out for insects to eat.

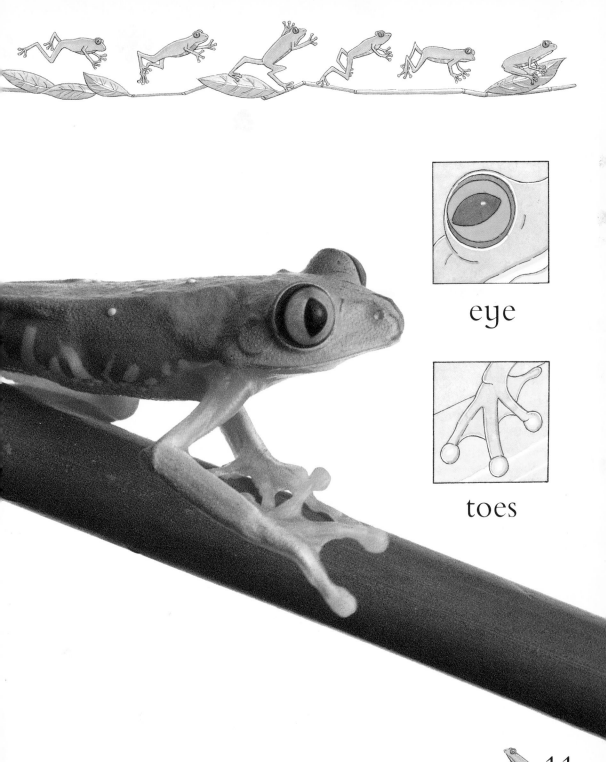

eye

toes

Crocodile

Crocodiles live near rivers or swamps and spend a lot of time in the water. Their powerful tails help them swim. Crocodiles use their jaws to snap up fish and other animals.

tail

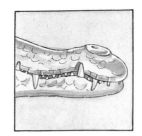

scales   teeth

eye

Orangutan

An orangutan is a big ape with very long arms. It uses them to swing from branch to branch through the trees. Orangutans eat fruit and blossoms. Every night they make a nest from leaves and branches.

arm

hand

15

Toucan

Toucans are noisy birds
that live in groups. They
build nests in the treetops.
Toucans use their giant
beaks to pick berries and
slice up soft, juicy fruits.

beak

eye   feather

Iguana

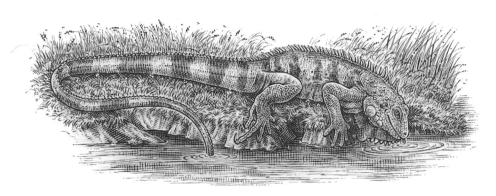

An iguana is a large lizard. It has thick, scaly skin. Iguanas eat leaves, flowers, and seeds. They are good swimmers and climbers. Every morning they climb high into the treetops to warm up in the sunshine.

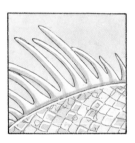

crest

tail

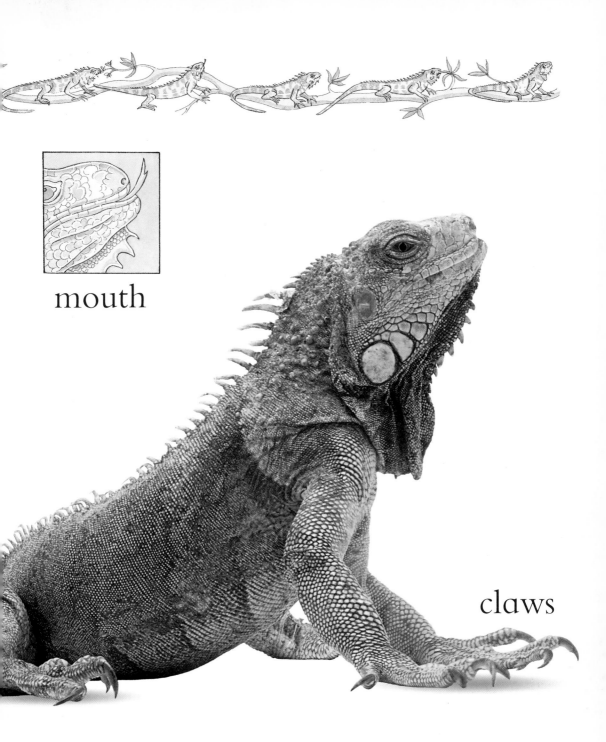

mouth

claws

19

Sloth

Sloths spend most of their time hanging upside down in trees. They can't walk! They grip tree branches with their hooked claws as they move slowly along. Sloths eat leaves and buds. Mother sloths carry their babies on their tummies.